Casting Down Imaginations

by

Don Shorter, Sr.

Casting Down Imaginations

by
Don Shorter, Sr.

Casting down imaginations, and every high thing that exalteth itself against the knowledge of God, and bringing into captivity every thought to the obedience of Christ.

2 Corinthians 10:5

2nd Printing
Over 10,000 in Print

Casting Down Imaginations
ISBN 0-88144-1
Copyright © 1991 by Don Shorter Ministries
P. O. Box 44051
Tacoma, WA 98444

Published by Harrison House, Inc.
P. O. Box 35035
Tulsa, Oklahoma 74153

Printed in the United States of America.

Dedication

This book is dedicated to my wife who prayed me out of a carnal Christian lifestyle. Her loving dedication, support, encouragement and source of challenge have been a real asset to all that God has called me to be.

Thank you, Kathy, for praying me to victory.

Contents

Special Thanks

My thanks to Barbara Anderson who put in countless hours of word processing and typing of the manuscript of this book for nearly two years, as well as my loving wife, Kathy Shorter, for her spirit of excellence and encouragement in helping to edit and proofread this book, and especially to God the Father and His Son Jesus for allowing me to receive this revelation through His precious Holy Spirit.

To the readers of Casting Down Imaginations:

This book is designed to be read slowly and prayerfully. Please do not speed read this book. Study, meditate and apply the steps and illustrations to your life to begin a new lifestyle of victory on a daily basis.

Foreword

This book is a message of truth that will help you walk in God's will and plan for your life. So many Christians struggle through life and never achieve the full potential of their life. The reasons are addressed in the following pages. Pastor Shorter will help you overcome the things that can paralyze your life.

You will be encouraged and motivated to win in life as you read these pages. The truth in them will make you free.

Casey Treat
Seattle, Washington

In bringing light to a darkened world, we must first know and live the power of God in our body, mind and spirit before we can impart to others. Obtaining the revelation of God's plan for us, we can then be strenthened by the Holy Spirit to perform what God has commissioned.

In John 10:10 it says, *"The thief cometh not, but for to steal, and to kill, and to destroy: I am come that they might have life, and that they might have it more abundantly."* The first place of attack is usually in our minds and we combat it by choosing to cast it down by the mighty Word of God.

"Casting Down Imaginations" is for every Christian who is serious about yielding themselves to the Holy Spirit so they may grow in Him and live their lives victoriously!

Henry Hinn
Vancouver, Canada

Introduction

Every person goes through change, either negative or positive. Change is always occurring. To grow and become more effective for the Kingdom of God, positive change must especially occur.

When you are born again (become a Christian), you experience a spiritual change instantaneously. This is done by asking Jesus to be Lord of your life and accepting Him as your Lord and Savior, according to Romans 10:9,10. The Word of God simply states that if anyone will confess Jesus as Lord of his life and believe that God raised Jesus from the dead, he will be saved. Once you have done this, you are *born* into God's kingdom, and become a child of God.

The Bible declares that once you become a Christian, you are a new creature: ''Behold, all things are become new.'' You pass from death to life immediately. However, there are two other areas that being born again does not immediately change: 1) Your soul (your mind, will and emotions), and 2) your physical body (the flesh). These areas become two of the hottest battlegrounds for the remainder of your life, and it will become more and more evident that the ''soulish'' part of your life (the *mind, will* and *emotions* will become the area of the enemy's *focus* for attack. It is *learning* how to overcome in these areas through God's Word that we will focus upon throughout this book.

Once we accept Jesus as Lord and Savior, we are born of the Holy Spirit, Who seals us until the day of redemption. At this point, our lives take on a whole new meaning. We have a new outlook on life and a new Lord to serve. The Apostle Paul stated it this way:

For I delight in the law of God after the inward man,

But I see another law in my members, warring against the law of my mind, and bringing me into captivity to the law of sin which is in my members.

O wretched man that I am! Who shall deliver me from the body of this death?

I thank God through Jesus Christ our Lord....
Romans 7:22-25

Jesus is our deliverer.

We see two laws at work within us. Our "inward man," or spirit man, delights or seeks after the law of God, but there is another law at war *against* the law of our *mind*. This battle is waged in the *mind* of the believer, as well as the unbeliever, 24 hours per day, 7 days per week, 365 days per year. Thank God, the believer's mind can be settled through the *Spirit of God (the Holy Spirit)* and *faith* in *the Word of God.*

God Our Deliverer

Our bodies naturally desire to *fulfill* the lusts of the world, while our recreated human spirits desire to *go* the way of God. In the Bible Paul says that *God* will deliver us from this dilemma through Jesus Christ our Lord.

In 2 Corinthians 10:3-5, the warfare we wage in our mind is further explained by the Apostle Paul:

> For though we walk in the flesh, we do not war after the flesh:
>
> (For the weapons of our warfare are not carnal, but mighty through God to the pulling down of strongholds;)
>
> *Casting down imaginations, and every high thing that exalteth itself against the knowledge of God, and bringing into captivity every thought to the obedience of Christ.*

In 2 Corinthians 10:4,5, we will begin to see and understand the strategy God has given us in His Word to win this battle for control of the soul. Throughout this book, we will examine an effective process designed for us to have the proper weapons deployed at any given time in our life to help us cast down negative imaginations and bring every thought into obedience to Christ. Our weapons are given to us by God, according to Ephesians 6:14-17:

> Stand therefore, having your loins girt about with *truth,* and having on the *breastplate of righteousness;*
>
> And your feet shod with the preparation of the *gospel of peace;*
>
> Above all, taking the *shield of faith,* wherewith ye shall be able to quench all the fiery darts of the wicked.
>
> And take the *helmet of salvation,* and the *sword of the Spirit,* which is the *word of God.*

Our main focus will be on the *sword of the Spirit,* which is the *Word of God.* As we do this, we will become equipped to analyze any thought that exalts itself above the knowledge of God and His best for our life. By doing this we will find that every thought will become naked and open for our examination.

Hebrews 4:12 says: For *The Word of God is* quick (alive) and powerful, and sharper than *any* twoedged sword, piercing even to the dividing asunder of *soul* and *spirit,* and of the joints and marrow, *and is a discerner of the thoughts and intents of the heart.* Neither is there *any creature* that is not manifest *in His sight:* But all things are naked and opened unto the eyes of him with whom we have to do.[7]

1
We Are Redeemed From the Curse

Many believers have the attitude that once they are born again they have escaped becoming a target for the enemy, but they have not. To understand this situation, let me have you think on this example for a moment. When a wild animal is born in the forest, the job of the parents is to protect and feed this newborn creature during every moment of its very early existence. The forest is filled with nourishment as well as predators waiting for an opportunity to take advantage of the carelessness of the parents or the curiousness of the newborn. Many may say, *"It's a jungle out there,"* but in reality it is just *warfare in the day-to-day lifestyle in the animal kingdom.* This example graphically depicts the life of the Christian from the *spiritual* point of view.

Because of Adam's transgression (Gen. 3:17), the world has been cursed, and with it, man and woman, making it in many ways a jungle. *Remember, whenever you see the word "curse," you must put into your mind that it means nothing good at all.* However, as believers, we are *redeemed* from that curse by the blood of Jesus.

Christ hath redeemed us (bought us out of and) **from the curse of the law, being made a curse for us:**

17

for it is written, cursed is every one that hangeth on a tree:

That the blessing of Abraham might come on the Gentiles through Jesus Christ; that we might receive the promise of the Spirit through faith.

Galatians 3:13,14

As a believer, you are no longer under a curse. You are blessed (fortunate, one to be envied).

Jesus Christ became that curse and died on the cross for the sins of the whole world. But even though Jesus died on the cross for the sins of the world, that did not take away the curse for the *entire* world. It was only for those living in the world who accept His sacrifice on the cross (tree). This means we must day in and day out deal with those of the world still under the influence of the curse, even though we are personally redeemed from the curse of this world.

You and I have been given weapons to *win* the battle against the enemy in the jungle out there. It's up to us to learn how to deploy the weapons we have been given by God.

God's Weapons Are Mightier

Satan is known as the god of this world. He will try to come after us with his own weapons. However, as we just read in 2 Corinthians 10:4,5, these weapons given to believers are not carnal (or of this world), but they are mighty through God and they have a definite purpose... *to pull down the enemy's strongholds.* As we read in this passage,

(...to the pulling down of strong holds;)

Casting down imaginations, and *every* **high thing that exalteth** *itself* **against the knowledge of God**....

Before we begin to cast down any thing, we must know by what authority we are to cast down these high things that exalt themselves above the knowledge of God (His will and purpose in our lives).

In this passage the Bible states that the weapons to which every believer has access are mighty. We are only mighty through God, not through ourselves or the might of others. Simply put, *we are to cast down anything that exalts itself above the knowledge of God's will and purpose for us.*

To further understand this concept, let me explain what the will of God is and is not. The will of God is *expressed in the Word of God, the Bible, and the Bible must become the final* authority on any subject in life as well as the guide for casting down or exalting anything. Christians must begin to analyze the environment around them. They must examine their environment in relationship to their accepted faith in God's Word in order to understand His *will* for every part of their life. Just as the newborn creature of the forest, we must rely upon our heavenly Father to learn what will be helpful or harmful to us as we focus on His will for us as expressed in His Word.

For many Christians, this process does not begin properly. Religious traditions, sectarian barriers, cares of this world, etc. stop them from being *fed* or from being *led* by God's Word, and they become confused, frustrated and defeated. Christians become instant lunch for their enemy, falling prey to his wicked vices and devices, and are *slowly* taken back into the jungle of this world as Satan's trophies.

19

For other Christians, the process begins quickly, but then stops at a certain level of growth, after they feel they have arrived spiritually or materially. But to assure *continued* spiritual growth in the midst of the cursed world in which we live, we must continue to learn how to cast down the thoughts that Satan presents to our minds and exalt the Word of God in every situation.

Your Life Is Being Shaped

Receiving information, opinions, teachings, doctrines, arguments or lifestyles will begin to shape the life and *habit* patterns of any person in this world. When we are *physically born* into this world, we immediately begin to be shaped by those around us. Opinions, ideas, suggestions, doctrines, arguments, all come to the mind of a person and must be analyzed, sorted, accepted, rejected, or replaced. All of these decisions work as building blocks in a person's growth.

There is no difference when we are spiritually born again. The input we *receive* will determine our growth in every aspect of life.

I remember the conception and birth of each of our children. Each time, as soon as my wife and I learned that she was pregnant, we began praying for our new baby, speaking life to each one while it was only days into conception in my wife's womb. We would begin telling them they were blessed, smart, prosperous and healthy according to the Word of God, even though my wife was only days or weeks past conception. We continued throughout the pregnancy until each one was born already *shaped* in the words of faith spoken before they were ever seen. (This includes our present unborn child now in his ninth month of conception, ready to be born any day.)

Death and life are in the power of the tongue....
Proverbs 18:21

You will live or die by the words you receive, accept and exalt over your life as well as the words *you speak* over your life.

Every day of your life you will be presented with hundreds upon hundreds of thoughts, ideas, and suggestions to your mind by outside sources. To every one of us, Christian or non-Christian alike, these thoughts will be presented. For example, today you will be presented with a number of suggestions by billboards, signs, bumper stickers, radio, television and telephone propositions, as well as memories from the past, and images of the future, some good, some bad, some true, some false, but *you* will decide what you will believe and exalt in your life. You are controlling this part of your life, no one else is, *not even God.*

God gave you the authority and control over this area, and you are the determining factor. All of these influences are consistently in the process of suggesting things to the human imagination, some good, and some detrimental to your growth as a mature person and certainly as a successful Christian.

To live a successful Christian life, this state of the mind must be checked constantly to help you to receive the information most needed to operate effectively in today's society. This problem cannot be solved by living your life with your senses closed off. You must understand that you are going to be *presented* with negative information no matter how holy and sanctified you are. (I am not trying to be arrogant; it's just a fact.)

The key to living in victory is also to remember that your thoughts are controlled by the input *you* allow to be received and accepted as truth and exalted as the standards in your life.

In Proverbs 23:7, we read that a person is determined by his thoughts,

> **For as he thinketh in his heart, so is he....**

The Bible also says of Jesus,

> **...as he is, so are we in this world.**
>
> I John 4:17

Catch ahold of this truth and never forget it: *To be presented with a thought, suggestion or idea is one thing; but what you do with that thought, suggestion or idea is another totally different thing. It will determine your entire future: physically, mentally and spiritually.* Remember, you are the deciding factor. You make the decision to accept it or reject it.

Years ago, my wife and I became hooked on soap operas. This may seem like a very small thing at first, but in reality we were opening ourselves up to be *trained* in a lifestyle we did not want. As time went on, we discussed, studied and somewhat lived the lives of the characters displayed on our television screen in our own home. Many Christians do not understand why watching, listening and following the lives of people living a lifestyle of sin, adultery, fornication, lies and cheating on television for perhaps three hours a day, five days a week, can negatively affect their lives. We did not know, until our eyes were refocused to the Word of God.

One day I heard someone say that the person I will become within the next few years will be determined by the books I read, the things I listen to and the people I associate with today.

> He that walketh with wise men shall be wise: but a companion of fools shall be destroyed.
>
> Proverbs 13:20
>
> Make no friendship with an angry man; and with a furious man thou shalt not go:
>
> Lest thou learn his ways, and get a snare to thy soul.
>
> Proverbs 22:24,25

As I began to look over my life and compare it to the Word of God and His will for me, I noticed that my reading, listening, and associating during my young Christian life was all on a very negative basis in comparison to the lifestyle (conversation) described in the Word of God. I also noticed that I was being snared and destroyed. No one had told me that it is Satan who destroys. I thought (because I was taught at a church I went to) that it was God just putting me through test after test to make me strong (even though I was getting weaker by the minute). Little did I know that I was *agreeing* to destroy myself by listening to and studying Satan's lifestyle and allowing him to train my mind, choose the words of my mouth, and ultimately control my deeds.

> This I say therefore, and testify in the Lord, that ye henceforth walk not as other Gentiles walk, in the vanity of their mind.
>
> Ephesians 4:17

Notice, there is supposed to be a difference in the walk (meaning the daily lifestyle) of the believer versus the unbeliever. The word in the Greek here for Gentile actually means a person without God and with no hope in the world. However, the walk for both the believer and unbeliever begins in the mind (with the purposes of the thoughts) determining the direction of the person's walk toward God's will or away from God's will.

As believers, we are to be aware of our state of mind at all times. In our daily walk, as we receive information the world is giving out, we must have a *different* state of mind.

God's Army

In 2 Timothy 2:4, Paul writes to Timothy,

> **No man that warreth entangleth himself with the affairs of this life; that he may please him who hath chosen him to be a soldier.**

Once we are born again, we are automatically inducted into the army of the Lord. We are commanded not to become entangled in the affairs of this world. That does not mean we do not live in the world. It simply means we must *remember* who we are while we are in it. You are a soldier *chosen* by God and on duty 24 hours per day. Make a decision to begin to learn who you are in God's army and how to use your mighty weapons of God to receive the victory Jesus has won for us.

Begin by reading, studying and praying about who you are in Christ. Watch and listen to programs that teach and preach about who you are in Christ. Listen to tapes that help you to know who you are in Christ. And most of all, get into a Bible-teaching church that will help you know who you are in Christ. You will begin to see your life take a turn for the better as never before as you begin to apply the principles of God's Word to your life.

> **My people are destroyed for lack of knowledge: because thou hast rejected knowledge, I will also reject thee, that thou shalt be no priest to me: seeing thou hast forgotten the law of thy God, I will also forget thy children.**
>
> **Hosea 4:6**

Knowledge of God's law (His Word) is so important to ensure victory for you. If you don't learn to exalt God's law, Satan will *force* his law upon you.

2
How You See Yourself

So far, we have established that it is a fact that everyone is presented with negative information.

Now, let's look at 2 Corinthians 10:5 again, but let's focus on the word "imaginations."

Casting down *imaginations*, and every high thing that exalteth itself against the knowledge of God, and bringing into captivity every thought to the obedience of Christ.

The Bible states in Genesis 1:27 that God created man in His own image. As a result, man became the highest being created in this earth realm. He was made a little lower than the angels. The word *"imagination"* can be broken down this way, *image — a — nation*. We read earlier that the Bible states: *"As a man thinketh in his heart so is he."* This really has to do with the imagination of a person. The image of a person is one of the most important indicators for his growth toward or away from God. Along with this self-concept is his view of self-worth and general belief in success. How you image (or imagine) yourself determines whether you please God or not. It also will determine whether you will be successful in life or not. I'm not talking about mind science or anything like that. I am talking about what the Bible says!

God's View of Man

In Numbers 13:33, the children of Israel were faced with entering Canaan and taking what God had said belonged to them. God had called the children of Israel strong and courageous, and had told them that He had given them the land of their enemies that flowed with milk and honey. God said that it was a good land, and that they should have it as His children. God said He would fight for them, and that they were to go up and take the land that He had promised them.

Of course, if God said it, He had to fulfil His promise because He cannot lie. However, they imagined themselves (before anyone else imagined them) as grasshoppers, entirely out of line from the way God had imagined and then spoken them to be. This scripture states that they saw themselves as grasshoppers, and because of this poor self-image (poor in comparison to what God said they were) or self-pity, they were grasshoppers in their enemies' sight as well.

And there we saw the giants, the sons of Anak, which come of the giants: and we were in our own sight as grasshoppers, and so we were in their (the enemy's) **sight.**

Numbers 13:33

This view began in their own mind and reflected what they thought of themselves, which was not at all according to the way God had seen them or spoken of them. God called them His own children, and of course God had not made grasshoppers of His sons and daughters created in His own image!

This negative view the people had of themselves displeased the Lord and caused the children of Israel to wander on a 40-year trail, murmuring against God and His chosen leaders. Can you imagine someone calling God's children grasshoppers? Ironically, this scripture clearly shows who started the name-calling, and it was not the enemies of God. It was the children of God who first thought of themselves as grass-hoppers, then began to speak what they were thinking in their hearts. When you do this, it makes it so easy for your enemies to agree and to begin to set your words into motion.

Your Self-Image

Remember, death and life are in the power of the tongue. (Prov. 18:21.) How you imagine yourself as a believer is so very important. It will determine how others think of you, and whether you please God or not. So many times we hear people talk about working on their self-image. However, the only true way for anyone to work on his self-image is to look at the manufacturer's manual. The manufacturer and the creator of all mankind is God, our Father, through our Lord Jesus Christ, in Whose image man was made. (Col. 1:15.) Any image or imagination of yourself that is not *based* on the manufacturer's manual (the Word of God) is an incorrect image.

As a believer, it is important for you to know who you are in Christ. You must be ready at all times to receive words said about you that concur with the Word of God, as well as be ready to cast down any imagination about yourself that is not according to the Word of God. The Bible is your guide for your self-image.

In order for you to receive more abundantly from God, speak the Word of God, exalt the Word of God so that the Holy Spirit working in you will cause you to receive what you are speaking and believing. Begin to meditate and picture what God's Word says you are, and what you can do in Christ.

Unchecked Thoughts

When it comes to receiving and submitting to negative thoughts, we must learn to cast down the past, including any thoughts gone unchecked about past failures or successes that are diametrically opposed to the Word of God. They are potentially dangerous to our spiritual well-being.

For many Christians the imagination of something negative happening to them has the ability of paralyzing them in such a way as to *give* place to fear. If not cast down, these negative thoughts or imaginations will come back again and again, holding the victim prisoner in his own mind. The root cause of worry is fear, and the root cause of fear is an *unchecked imagination* and lack of knowledge of the Word of God.

The Bible states in 2 Timothy 1:7, **For God hath not given us the spirit of fear; but of power, and of love, and of a sound mind.** If God gives a sound mind, then Satan, who is opposed to God, must be the one who is giving the *spirit of fear*. It is up to you to make the decision to arrest those negative thoughts and cast them down by the Word of God. God will not do it for you. He has already given you the authority to do so. Begin to *arrest* those negative thoughts; cast down those negative imaginations now.

Carnality

For the weapons of our warfare are not carnal....
2 Corinthians 10:4

That word "carnal" needs to be explained. Have you ever heard of "chili con carne"? The word "Carne" means meat or flesh. The weapons of our warfare are not carnal or of the flesh. They are not according to our brain power or intellect with the ability relying on the physical senses, "I'll figure this one out myself." Neither are they of the feelings of the flesh, "I feel victorious." That is not what they are. What are they? They are "mighty through God to the pulling down of strongholds." We'll discuss what a stronghold is later, but understand this: Your weapons that God has given to you are mighty; they are not carnal, and you must understand how to use them to live victoriously.

Ruled By the Law of Lasciviousness

Who being past feeling have given themselves over unto lasciviousness, to work all uncleanness with greediness.
Ephesians 4:19

When carnal efforts are in the *forefront* of the battles of a born-again person, the ultimate state of existence and lifestyle are based on lawlessness. Lawlessness (or taking your life into your own hands) is the spirit of the world. The Bible clearly calls this attitude lasciviousness or lawlessness. This word, however, *cannot be applied to a person who is not born again and is still living according to the world, because people of the world do what they want to do without restraint, by the very nature of their existence. However, when this carnal state of mind*

31

takes over a believer's life, allowing certain things to continue, this unchecked state of existence is described as lasciviousness. Simply defined, it means a lack of restraint, first in thoughts, then in words, and ultimately in deeds. Thoughts are seeds, and seeds are going to come up someday if they are planted consistently in the right conditions. If a person keeps putting the wrong things in his physical body (i.e., drugs, alcohol, unhealthy foods, etc.), eventually negative effects will show up, no matter how much faith he may have that they won't.

Everyone has certain weaknesses of the flesh that the enemy knows about. For some of us it may be a chemical dependency, some kind of drug or alcohol. For others, it may be lust or the love of money. But whatever this weakness, we must understand that God has given us weapons to use to combat those things working against us. Those desires left unchecked and never restrained will cause that person to end up living a life overrun by a state of mind ruled by the law of lasciviousness. There are some Christians who are totally out of control — either in their finances, body, homes or imaginations. These things are overgrowing their lives. They may have accepted Christ. They may be going to heaven, but they have no control over their present lives.

The opposite of lasciviousness is excellence. Excellence says, "I am not going to put up with sloppiness, laziness and lack of constraint. I am not going to have those kinds of negative thoughts ruling my life." Only you, the believer, can break the power of the devil over your thoughts. You make the decision.

What will it be, excellence or lasciviousness? You choose.

Thoughts Must Be
Planted First

Satan desires to bombard your mind through *every* means possible: radio, television, newspaper, any way he can. However, without the incubation process of negative imaginations and thoughts, he cannot effectively cause your life to be changed by these bombardments. Satan *can't* put you in a neck hold and pull you down to a bar and get you drunk. He first suggests the idea. He may use anyone, perhaps someone you believe is a friend. Remember, the thought must always be planted first. Many Christians *silently* deal with areas of temptation and bombardment in their minds, while trying to cover them up from people around them.

Remember, 2 Corinthians 10 states that the weapons of *our* warfare are not carnal. *We are in a war,* and the enemy is constantly trying to attack his opponents; and may I remind you that you are his opponent, if you are on God's side. The only way to *win* this battle against our opponent is to remember that when it comes to regulating the thoughts in our minds, we must learn to compare everything — and I do mean everything (thought, word or deed) — with the Word of God. If it is below the standard of the Word, we must immediately cast it down.

Imaginations and perceptions are very powerful. We can see this in children who watch a steady diet of Saturday morning cartoons. They can see themselves in the imagination that has been placed in their minds by the television. I have seen this time and time again, not only with children, but adults. For 15 years I had a career in the media, particularly in television and radio, and I have seen clearly the effect that imagination and perceptions tainted in one way or another has had upon well-meaning people. The secular media uses the power of suggestion to its advantage very effectively to make a profit and to sell ideas, concepts, services and lifestyles to anyone who will listen or watch and do. Many people find themselves meditating or muttering the ideas, concepts, or logos of someone's company without any awareness of what has been done to their thought process.

With all this influence upon us, I am not saying that we should be paranoid about everything in the media, nor am I saying that everything in the media is satanically derived, but I personally know first-hand how imaginations can be used to *change* habit patterns and lifestyles and people through just suggesting an idea at the right time.

Let's look at Genesis 2:17. God is speaking to Adam regarding the trees of the garden:

But of the tree of the knowledge of good and evil, thou shalt not eat of it: for in the day that thou eatest thereof thou shalt surely die.

That statement seems very clear, doesn't it? Let's look at Genesis 3:1. The serpent Satan, is speaking here questioning Eve about what God told Adam:

Now the serpent was more subtle than any beast of the field which the Lord God had made. And he said unto the woman, Yea, *hath God said,* Ye shall not eat of every tree of the garden?

Two things are wrong with the interrogation. Why is the serpent asking Eve what God said? She was not there. Adam was. Secondly, why is the serpent questioning God? Certainly not for more clarification for himself. These are two very important keys.

And the woman said unto the serpent, We may eat of the fruit of the trees of the garden:

But of the fruit of the tree which is in the midst of the garden, God hath said, Ye shall not eat of it, neither shall ye touch it, lest ye die.

(God did not say, "You shall not touch it, lest you die." Eve misunderstood.) In verse 4, notice this:

And the serpent said unto the woman, Ye shall not surely die.

Stop right there and let's go back to Genesis 2:16,17:

And the Lord God commanded the man, saying, Of every tree of the garden thou mayest freely eat:

But of the tree of the knowledge of good and evil, thou shalt not eat of it: for in the day that thou eatest thereof thou shalt surely die.

Now, who is the liar here? Satan is, of course, as always. The distortion of the truth was and will always be Satan's tactic to steal your blessings from you. The enemy cannot steal outright anything from you without your permitting it. He has to *deceive* you out of what God has given you in order for you to lose it, either through ignorance of God's Word, or nonappropriation of the Word of God that you do know.

Now let's look at the consequences of not knowing what God really said and what He meant when He said it.

And when the woman *saw* that the tree was good for food, and that it was pleasant to the eyes, and a tree to be desired to make one wise, she took of the fruit thereof, and did eat....

Genesis 3:6

Clearly this scripture shows that the woman began to imagine or see new ideas (though they transgressed God's Word). This imagination set itself up against the knowing of God or the knowledge of God's Word spoken directly to Adam. By following this imagination and allowing it to be exalted in the perception of her mind, Eve and her husband were separated from their former relationship with God.

Satan's plan is to *keep* us in a state of negative imaginations for three main reasons: guilt, condemnation and ultimate separation from God. He wants to keep us wrapped up in our own circumstances and problems. You *must* begin to analyze every word and determine if it exalts itself above the knowledge of God. What you take into your mind, your heart and your ears is very important. Don't let anyone dump any garbage on you. Learn to be *always* conscious of what you are receiving.

3
The Power That Works in You

There is a powerful force waiting inside of you. **Now unto him that is able to do exceeding abundantly above all that we ask or think, according to the power that *worketh in us*** (Eph. 3:20). "Now unto him." Who is Him? Him *means* Him: God, Jesus, the Holy Spirit. He is able. Whatever you are asking, God is able to do exceeding abundantly above that (if it is in line with His Word, His Will). Whatever your situation is, whatever you are dealing with, God is able to do exceeding abundantly above what you could possibly ask or think. Look at 1 Corinthians 2:9:

> **. . . Eye hath not seen, nor ear heard, neither have *entered in the heart of man, the things which God* hath prepared for them that love him.**

Some Christians try to think of themselves *above* what the Word of God says about them, while at the same time all too often God's people think way *below what the Word of God says about them* and what God's promises are for them in His Word. "Both are equally wrong.

As an example, think of the Word of God as a paved road. Those who are walking firmly on the road's surface could be considered those walking firmly on the Word of God. Unfortunately, there are, however, always some people who, in spite of all that the Word of God says about them, still choose to walk below what the Word of God says about them, living by their feelings with thoughts of worthlessness and defeat. The reason they feel this way many times is based on their own *unregulated* thoughts causing them to live their lives contrary to the Word of God.

Think on this for a moment. Where are sewer pipes usually located? Underneath the ground, below the road's surface. There is a reason for this, mainly because sewage is waste, good for nothing and very unpleasant to deal with. Sewage is something that is no longer any good. We should not allow the sewage of the world's thinking and ways of our past to run through our minds. You'll perhaps hear people saying: "God is just giving all this to me to humble me," or perhaps, "I'll never make it, I'm just a loser," or "I'll never get ahead, I'll always be poor." Don't say that! That's not true. That may be your imagination or the thoughts or imagination of others about you, but that's not what the Word of God says about you.

"Now unto him that is able to do exceeding abundantly above all that we ask or think." What are you asking? What are you thinking? If you were asked about your finances, what would you say about that area? Would it be according to the Word of God, or according to your present circumstances, or someone's opinion? If you were asked about your children, if you were asked about your job or business or your ability in ministry, if you were asked about what is happening in your spiritual life, would your thoughts go down to the sewer, or could they be on the road (the Word of God)?

God has given you the *ability* to ascend to His Word, rise up to the level of His Word, and receive from His Word. Don't try to live above it and certainly not below it. Live in it and walk on it! That guarantees a solid foundation for success!

Look at the last part of this scripture again, "above all that we can ask or think according to the *power* that worketh in us." That is the Word of God. God is able to do exceeding abundantly above what you ask or think according to the power that is working in you. If God's power is what is going to do it (that is, exceed your thoughts or requests), then all you have to do is *put your faith to work* and *believe to receive.* Don't worry about it! *Receive it.* Don't cry about it, *receive it.* Don't try to explain it away, just have faith and be ready to receive it. Expect to receive exceeding abundantly above what you are asking or thinking.

God is the One Who is going to deliver it to you, according to His power that works in you. So don't hinder the power working in you; don't be fearful of the power working in you. Let God's power have free reign to work in you, beginning right now.

Receive God's Free Gift

If you don't have the power of God working in you, that is the reason there may be very little going on around you. The Spirit of God is inside of you working with your thoughts and carrying out your words to create for you the promises of God for every part of your life. As we read earlier, the Holy Spirit is what is working with you and in you.

Satan knows that when a person receives this gift of the Holy Spirit, that individual will be equipped with supernatural power. Without the power of the Holy Spirit and faith in God's Word, it's hard to receive any of God's promises. Look at your life right now and ask yourself this question: What is working in me? Is the Holy Spirit working in you? Or are the imaginations of fear, worry, the past, sin and negative thoughts of the world working in you? You have the power to cast down those imaginations that are crowding God's promises out of your mind and to exalt the knowledge of God in your life.

The Bible says that the Holy Spirit will guide you, and will lead you into all truth, and will cause you to receive from God His direction and counsel. It is literally *impossible* for you to cast down imaginations and the negative things that come to your mind without the Holy Spirit's power and discerning and leading. You can't effectively do this by yourself by saying, ''Well, I cast that down; I cast this down,'' randomly under your own power. It must be done by the power of God given to you, and that power must be working in you.

Every time you receive a thought, you must determine if the thought is in line with God's will (His Word) or not. It is confusing just to say, ''That is negative; I don't believe that; I shouldn't accept that,'' without a standard. The *standard* you use must *always* be the knowledge of God's Word and the assistance of the Holy Spirit to bring it to your remembrance. You see, casting down a negative thought, fear or imagination is one thing, but eventually you must *fill* that emptiness with something. *You will ultimately exalt someone's words in your life.* To properly replace those negative thoughts, you must replace them with the Word of God; not religious tradition, or the opinions of others, but the Word of God.

> **In the last day, that great day of the feast, Jesus stood and cried, saying, If any man thirst, let him come unto me, and drink.**
>
> **He that believeth on me, [is a believer] as the scripture hath said, out of his belly shall flow rivers of living water.**
>
> **But this spake he of the Spirit, which they that believe on him should receive: for the Holy Ghost was not yet given; because that Jesus was not yet glorified.**
>
> **John 7:37,39**

Some think that the world's counselors are the only ones who are going to be able to help them. Some think that medical doctors are going to come up with all they need for every ailment of their bodies. Thank God for the doctors, but it is the Holy Spirit we need. He is the power source that God has given us to overcome in *every* situation: body, soul and spirit. God has given you and me a Helper; His name is the Holy Spirit. Receive Him now. When you do, among many other things He will: 1) bring things to your remembrance (so that you will know how to replace those imaginations you cast down with the Word of God), 2) comfort you in every situation, and 3) guide you into all truth. You can't do this on your own power. We are not smart enough to handle these areas by ourselves.

Receive the Holy Spirit by asking according to Luke 11:13. After you ask, pray out as the Spirit gives you the utterance according to Acts 2:4. Open your mouth and allow the Lord to fill it. Now pray regularly in your new language according to Jude 20.

Hearing and Obeying
the Holy Spirit

God does not just want a part of you. He wants all of you including your mind, will and emotions. He wants your body. He wants your spirit. He wants everything you have. This is your reasonable service, and when you give yourself *totally* to Him, expect a return.

God wants you *all* of the time. There are not many wives who would live in a relationship where they spent time with their husband only once a week, and the rest of the week he was not their husband. If they were committed, they would expect the same commitment from their husband. Or visa versa, suppose that one day per week a husband had access to his wife, and for that one day per week she was totally faithful and committed to him but the rest of the week, forget it! We would not *expect* that relationship to last very long.

God is not looking for an uncommitted relationship with you. God is looking for a committed relationship in harmony with you. You control the ability to use your imagination to see yourself going somewhere and doing something great, or to see yourself defeated and in a rut. You control whether or not you see yourself in the Body of Christ the way that God has placed you to be. God has called you to do great things for Him, but it takes commitment. He has called you to do many great things, and you are the only one who can hold you back. God is not holding you back and the devil can't (he's been stripped of that authority by Jesus.)

Years ago, the only way I could start my car was by rolling it down a hill (any hill I could find close to where I was parked). I would put my car in gear and jump into it as it was rolling while jerking the clutch up quickly to start the engine. That was my lifestyle. This went on for many months.

After a period of time I began to learn that if I was going to change my circumstances (the way I was getting around), I was going to have to use my faith, be committed and believe what God said I could have according to His Word, not what I was imagining myself doing day after day. I had to *develop a vision and image of change.* I found a scripture to stand on and began to confess and believe for a new car over and above the imaginations of the present (pushing my car down hill after hill). I had to imagine myself with a brand new car that started on its own.

This seems to be a small thing to me now, but it wasn't a small thing to me then. I had to stand on the Word, confess what I wanted and believe I had received it the whole time I was pushing my car down hill after hill. Well, praise God! Shortly after that period of time, a miracle happened. I received a brand new car (that started on its own). I did not have to push my car any longer. This car came with a 100,000-mile warranty and was showroom fresh. To receive it, I had to believe that God desired for me to receive the desires of my heart (according to Psalm 37:4). I had to cast down the thoughts of pushing my car any longer. I had to see myself driving my old car to the dealership and driving off with a brand new car.

The Holy Spirit directed me one day to go to a certain new car dealer whom I had known years earlier.

By the Lord's direction, I drove right onto the lot and left that old clunker running while I negotiated for a new vehicle. Within an hour or so I drove off the lot with a brand new car. No more pushing, and no more embarrassment.

It is God's will for you to be blessed in every area of life. Wherever you are in your present situation in life, learn to cast down the thoughts that are holding you back from being blessed. God desires for His people to see themselves the way He does, and to live in obedience to His Word to receive His best.

> **If ye be willing and obedient, ye shall eat the good of the land.**
>
> **Isaiah 1:19**

Don't speak any of the negative imaginations that you have received from outside sources. Throw them down, pull them down, wrestle them down, cast them down. Put your foot on their neck and say: ''That is not me. That is not where I am going. That is not what I am going to do or be. I *refuse* to live the lifestyle being submitted to me. I take that thought captive now in the name of Jesus.'' Get violent with the negative thoughts that Satan is submitting to your mind. God has miracles waiting for you. Don't get used to the way things are. They can change for you.

Proverbs 19:21 says:

> **There are many devices in a man's heart; nevertheless the counsel of the Lord, that shall stand.**

God will allow us to receive second best if that is what we desire and want. But we don't have to *settle* for second best in any part of our lives. *Remember this, whatever we receive from Satan, even though it is his best, it is always second best to what God has planned for us. If* you catch hold of this principle, you will receive something that will change your life. You will never be the same. You will never think the way you have been thinking any more. You will think differently, with better thoughts.

Let's compare 2 Corinthians 10:5 with Genesis 6:5,6

> Casting down imaginations, and every high thing that exalteth itself against the knowledge of God, and bringing into captivity every thought to the obedience of Christ.
>
> 2 Corinthians 10:5

> And God saw that the wickedness of man was great in the earth, and that every imagination of the thoughts of his heart was only evil continually.
>
> And it repented the Lord that he had made man on the earth, and it grieved him at his heart.
>
> Genesis 6:5,6

That is the grieving of the Spirit of God. The Holy Spirit can be described as a gentleman, easily grieved by disobedience and vain imaginations. He will not push Himself on anyone. He only desires to work through willing vessels.

A few years ago, I watched a man campaigning for office. He had some pamphlets in his hand about his campaign and what he would do to help the residents of that community live better lives, if only given a chance. He was a very nice man. He was standing outside of a store waiting for people to go in or come out so he could talk to them. To the ones who were willing to listen, he would hand them his pamphlet and share his ideas and suggestions. Some people were just too busy or were going their own way too fast, because of that they couldn't be part of what he was talking about. Others moseyed on by, but when they saw him they looked away trying to ignore that he was there. Still he would try to hand them a pamphlet and they would walk by without even looking at him. Actually, they didn't want to meet him and didn't want his suggestions. Others would take his pamphlet and quickly shake his hand. They were so glad to meet him, and wanted to hear his suggestions.

That is how it is with the Holy Spirit. He would really like to have fellowship with us. Maybe it's early in the morning and a great time to spend time in prayer with the Holy Spirit. The Lord may say: "You need to spend a few minutes with Me. I have some things I want to share with you that will help you with your ministry, life, or business." We can just mosey on by in life trying to ignore Him, or else we can say: "Okay, Lord, tell me. What do You want me to know? How do You want to lead me?

God wants friendship, and fellowship heart to heart. He wants you to succeed. *He knows that you may have a lot of devices in your heart, but the plan that He has will stand.*

Some say that the Holy Spirit went away when the 12 apostles died. Others say that hearing from God was for years ago and not now. All the while, the Holy Spirit is here with the plan on how to change our life. It is up to us to receive Him. The man who was campaigning did not say, "If you don't agree with my thoughts or vote for me, I will punch your lights out." He just stood there. To those who would accept him, he would share his plan. Those who wouldn't were the losers, as far as his views were concerned.

Learn to cast down your plan, and exalt God's plan in your life. It will stand.

God has many thoughts and ideas for you that are just what you need. The Holy Spirit has many steps for you to take to be successful. His *first* requirement is for you to be a willing vessel.

4

Pulling Down of Strongholds in Your Mind

Many people need healing in their minds due to many reasons: perverted or unchecked sexual fantasies or actions, abuse in past relationships, broken promises or marriages, bad business experiences or career decisions bringing *images of failure* and poor self worth again and again into their minds. These people wear emotional scars. These scars can be removed even though they are not instantly wiped away when a person becomes born again. The reason is simple. When a person is born again, this experience does not immediately affect his mind, which is part of the soul.

The soul involves the mind, will and emotions. You are a three-part person. You are a spirit (made in the image of God). You possess a soul made up of your mind (intellect), your will (which *you* control) and your emotions. You live in a physical body.

As I stated in Chapter 1, your spirit is born again when you accept Jesus as your Lord and Savior. Your body is to be presented as a living sacrifice until it will be glorified when Jesus comes to meet us in the air. But according to Romans 12:1,2, your mind must be renewed to the Word of God:

> **I beseech you therefore, brethren, by the mercies of God, that ye present your bodies a living sacrifice,**

holy, acceptable unto God, which is your reasonable service.

And be not conformed to this world, *but be ye transformed by the renewing of your mind*, **that ye may prove what is that good, and acceptable, and perfect, will of God.**

The decision to renew your mind is one that *you* must make. It is a step that only *you* can take. This step involves learning how to cast down the negative thoughts you have received over the years, and replacing those thoughts with what the Bible says. This is a lifelong process.

Those dealing with scars must be willing to closely examine and finally reject those things not in line with God's Word, casting them down for good.

Research has shown that many prostitutes and child abusers have a history of being abused in childhood, leaving them with thoughts of unworthiness and self-condemnation. The past consistently haunts their minds, captivating them with the thoughts of being victimized in a lifestyle they never wanted. While the physical actions of the past may have long since passed, they remain *victimized* in their minds, their own imagination. Many of these abused people (Christian or non-Christian) turn into abusers themselves if the chain is not broken. But through the blood of Jesus Christ, the chain can be broken.

Maybe you or some one you know has been dealing with these types of problems. Understand this. You can learn how to cast down those thoughts that have kept you victimized. You have the power to cast down the imaginations that you are exalting in your mind by the power in the blood of Jesus, while breaking the curse of these actions.

God's Thoughts

In Jeremiah 29:11, God says:

> **For I know the thoughts that I think toward you, ɔaith thc Lord, thoughts of peace, and not of evil, to give you an expected end.**

What God thinks about us is so much more important than what we or others think. You may think that you are terrible; that you are dirty, unworthy, filthy and that nobody loves you. You may think that you are a mess, and maybe your lifestyle is. But you don't have to continue living that way any longer, because that is not what God thinks of you. He thinks, "If I could only get My children to see that I love them. If I could only get them to understand that I care for them." We think that God thinks the way we think. He does not.

Let's look at Verse 12:

> **Then shall ye call upon me, and ye shall go and pray unto me, and I will hearken unto you.**

God will listen to you right where you are. Maybe you are broke, totally bankrupt, backslidden, dealing with sickness or disease in your body or just emerging from a divorce. God is waiting to hear from you, to heal and deliver you. Once you understand that the thoughts that He has for you are of peace, not of evil, to give you an expected end, then you will realize how God really thinks about you.

Forsaking Thoughts

Let the wicked forsake his way, and the unrighteous man his thoughts....

Isaiah 55:7

If you are going to begin to cast down negative imaginations, then some of your thoughts must be *forsaken*. That may mean that you are going to have to throw out all the religious or worldly junk you have learned in the past over many years. That includes anything that is contrary to the Word of God. If that is the case, so be it. Throw it out and start replacing it with the Word of God as your foundation.

I remember a few years ago I was invited as a young preacher to help put together and teach at a conference along with a few other prominent ministers from various backgrounds. These meetings were going to be very different for a pastor I knew very well. He had been quite involved with a church group that had some very strong rules about whom he was to associate with outside of his denomination. Their rules were mere traditions of men, and not according to the Word of God. However he was invited, and accepted to come and speak.

This particular pastor had been so tied into tradition by a select group of men in his own denomination that for him to come and speak at a church that was not affiliated with his denomination was very uncomfortable for him. The day that this man was to arrive at the conference to speak would prove to be a real culture shock for him, because he had some very strong preconceived imaginations of what to expect. For him, this was one of the first times he had been around Christian people of different or nondenominational backgrounds. It was hard for him to accept what he was about to see, because he had been taught over a period of more than 20 years that his denomination was the only true church.

That evening he preached a powerful message about learning how to change, which he later shared was more about himself and what he was going through at that time. After ministering that evening to those whom he had been taught to preach against, and had imagined as being against him, he was completely amazed. Contrary to his own imagination the receptiveness to him was warm with no regard to his affiliation. The only battle he was having was in his *own* mind, not with any of his Christian brothers and sisters. He never imagined or expected this to happen.

I later found out that immediately after this conference he took a three-month sabbatical leave from his post as senior pastor to travel the country to find out what else he had been misinformed about. During this excursion he and his wife visited every type of Christ-centered church he could find from coast to coast, in search of truth. He later told of how he visited these churches, some meeting in barns, some meeting out in the field, others meeting in beautiful cathedrals and wonderful buildings with people of every race. During this time, he started to realize that what he had imagined about the entire Body of Christ, based on the opinions of a few others, was not true. The thoughts he had were incorrect. He began to cast them down, and replace them with the truth.

He expressed that he found out that it did not matter who the people were. After a lot of prayer, he decided to do two things. First, he apologized to his entire congregation for the many years of wrong preaching and teaching and asked for their forgiveness. Next, he announced his resignation from his post as senior pastor. That was a couple of bold steps. But he wanted to change, and he decided to make the first steps toward change.

Tradition Vs. God's Word

Your own imagination can take you down the wrong path while leading others with you if not constantly checked by the Word of God. In Mark 7:13 Jesus spoke of...

Making the word of God of none effect through your tradition, which ye have delivered: and many such like things do ye.

You can nullify the Word of God by following a lifestyle based on tradition. That means that all the preaching and teaching and studying you have received is rendered void if tradition has first place in your mind and heart over the Word of God.

We must ask ourselves: What am I doing and why? Is it because of tradition (versus a relationship with God) or habit, or because of what the Word of God says?

Self-Examination

Examine yourselves, whether ye be in the faith....

2 Corinthians 13:5

We are to consistently be in the mode of self-examination, not self-condemnation. The Word says to examine. Check yourself with the mirror of the Word of God all of the time. James 1:22-25 reads:

54

But be ye doers of the word, and not hearers only, deceiving your own selves.

For if any be a hearer of the word, and not a doer, he is like unto a man beholding his natural face in a glass (a mirror):

For he beholdeth himself, and goeth his way, and straightway forgetteth what manner of man *he was.*

But whoso looketh into the perfect law of liberty, (the Word of God) **and** *continueth therein,* **he being not a forgetful hearer, but a doer of the work, this man shall be blessed in his deed.**

Do you want your deeds to be blessed? Of course you do! Then learn to examine yourself, continue in the Word and be a doer of the Word.

God desires to bless your deeds, but that blessing will always be in relationship with the Word of God being exalted in your life.

Imagination of God

Perhaps your imagination of God is that of an Ebenezer Scrooge. That is the view that some of us have of God. That He is an old man with a long gray beard, all withered up, just looking around, waiting for someone to do something wrong so He can smack them with a club. That is not the proper view of God. If that is even close to the way you imagine your heavenly Father, cast down that imagination now, because that may very well be the reason your faith is not working. It is being canceled by your doubt of God's desire for you to prosper and succeed.

Your imagination about God must be changed before you can begin to cast down any negative thing that exalts itself against the knowledge of God.

The Word War

In Luke 4:18, the Bible says that Jesus came to heal the brokenhearted and to help those who are bruised. As I stated earlier, some of us have bruises on our minds. Our minds have not been bruised physically, although some of us have been physically abused, but for a lot of us it has just been thought processes that have been bruised. The world, Satan, ourselves and others have caused us to receive bruises in our minds. If we were to take a look in the Spirit at some of our minds, and our thinking process, we would see black and blue marks all over them.

Your ears may have been bombarded with statements like, *"I am leaving." "I quit." "You're nothing." "You'll never be anything." "It's terminal." "There is no recovery." "This is it, irreconcilable differences." "We'll always be poor." "People like you aren't welcome here." "You're the wrong color or nationality."*

We are in the process of a *word war* every day. You and I must begin to defend ourselves, in fact, go forward and get on the offensive in this word war. The word war that I am talking about goes on in your own mind every moment. Remember, 2 Corinthians 10:4: **"For the weapons of our warfare are not carnal....)."** (of the flesh). **When you try to take on the enemy who is a spirit being through your flesh, you have just handed yourself instant defeat. You can't win fighting that way.** *Fight* you must, but only in the Spirit to guarantee victory.

> **(For the weapons of our warfare are not carnal, but *mighty* through God to the pulling *down* of strongholds;)**

Casting down imaginations, and every high thing that exalteth itself against the knowledge of God....
2 Corinthians 10:4,5

In the fourth verse the Bible mentions strongholds. Those words are used to describe a fortified thought. A means of hanging on to a way of thinking, contrary to the Word of God. A stronghold really has very little to do in this context with anything physical. It has to do with the mental thought patterns of the soul (mind, will and emotions) going on in the mind. Each stronghold is built brick by brick and is left to cement together in the mind of the person *over* a period of time. Each thought serves as another image or brick in the mind of the person, until the thoughts all come together to form a stronghold. I call these strongholds *thought castles* (based on the root Greek meaning of the word). Once formed, and if *left alone*, they will become a hardened thought process that will withstand almost anything, even the Word of God, if allowed.

Somewhere, someone submitted to your mind the thoughts that make up what you believe. They were *built* in your *mind* brick by brick, thought by thought, until they were left to harden into a stronghold.

So then faith cometh by hearing....
Romans 10:17

Whatever you are constantly hearing, you are building faith for. Words are suggestions and images. The suggestions of the world go into your mind as well as the commandments of God's Word. They are planted into your heart and entertained by your thoughts. If you allow them to stay there to be fertilized, fortified, harbored and protected, they become strongholds. They determine the actions that you will take. All Satan has to do is to plant a suggestion, just one thought at a time, to begin to build a stronghold (a thought castle) in your mind. If it is not *uprooted as a thought,* it will *grow* into a stronghold, like a fortified castle. This thought castle serves as the protection of the things that exalt themselves against the knowledge (knowing) of God. Thought castles (strongholds) are impossible to remove through the flesh, because they are instituted by creative spiritual forces opposed to God; but they are *not* impossible to remove through the weapons of our warfare through God. That is the reason Paul in 2 Corinthians 10:5 spoke about casting down the imaginations before they become a stronghold. While they are *just* a thought, before they are an action, cast them down.

Some thoughts are secretly hibernated, protected and guarded in our minds for so long that they take over. It is similar to the greenhouse effect. We have kept them nice and warm with plenty of sunlight. All of those suggestions, those negative thoughts, seeds of defeat, failure, secret sins, and poor self-image. The imaginations are in our minds, incubating and growing. They eventually *crowd out* and *stand hard against* the knowledge of God and His Word.

I saw a movie once when I was a youngster growing up called ''The Blob.'' The blob was a jelly-like creature that begin as a small object no bigger than a fist, but left alone in the right conditions it grew and grew. First, it took over the room in the house where it was being stored. Then while being left unchecked, it took over the entire house. It continued and took over the neighborhood. Then it eventually began to overrun the entire city. That is when everyone in the city realized it was a problem, but it was too late. It had grown too big to handle.

That was a silly movie, but it is an appropriate analogy of what happens to the thoughts left unchecked in our minds. Imaginations will start to grow if *left* unchecked. The imaginations of man are either good, or they are evil. God destroyed the earth and all the inhabitants (except Noah and his family) for this very reason: The imagination of their thoughts was continually evil. In Genesis 6:5 the Bible doesn't say that God destroyed these people because of the way they looked. God did not destroy the whole earth because of the way they talked. God did not destroy the entire earth because of who they associated with. It was destroyed because of the imagination of the thoughts of people's heart.

What I am saying to you is that imaginations are so vital in the lives of those in God's creation, that God will once again have to destroy this whole world because of the same thing: the evil imaginations of the hearts of men.

Exalting the Word of God

As Christians, we must learn to cast down imaginations that are exalted above the Word of God.

And God saw that the wickedness of man was great in the earth, and that every imagination of the thoughts of his heart was only evil continually.
Genesis 6:5

Imaginations left unchecked will build strongholds which will keep you from God. An unchecked mind, an unchecked heart and an unchecked spirit will take you down to the level of the world quickly. You can't afford that.

Remember this: Once we are born again, Satan cannot change our spiritual destiny without our permission. The choice is made unless we decide otherwise; but he will continue to do anything to try to torment our minds. Here is an example:

Naaman was a Syrian warrior and a very strong man. He also was a leper. He went to visit the prophet Elijah to be healed. Elijah told him to dip into the muddy Jordan River seven times to be healed. Elijah told him that when he came out of the water the seventh time, he would be healed. Here is Naaman's response:

> **But Naaman was wroth, and went away, and said, Behold, I thought, He will surely come out to me, and stand, and call on the name of the Lord his God, and strike his hand over the place, and recover the leper.**
>
> **2 Kings 5:11**

I can imagine what the men around Naaman were saying: *"Sir, cast that thought down if you want to get healed. Your thought does not matter now; listen to the word of the prophet of God and be healed."* Finally, Naaman listened and obeyed and was healed just as the prophet said. If God says to do it one way, you may be saying, "I thought God would say that I should do it another way." Naaman was saying the same thing to himself. *If you want the benefits of what God has and does, you have to learn how to cast down your thoughts and do it His way.* His way is clearly spelled out in the Bible.

5

Every High Thing
That Exalts Itself

There are two main ways that the knowledge of God can be prevented from being received. First, by not being *acknowledged*. If I put a $1,000 bill in the back of this book and you did not acknowledge that it was real, if you thought it was money from a Monopoly game, you would not go out and try to spend it. That is the same way some people hear the message of the Gospel. They do not acknowledge and receive it for themselves. The second way the knowledge of God is prevented from being received is by *ignorance. Some people just have never heard the message of the good news.*

Herod and the Word

Let's take a look at a graphic example of what happened to a person who exalted himself against the knowledge of God. King Herod had beheaded James, the brother of John. This made him very popular with his followers who enjoyed this type of punishment against Christians. (What a strange way to receive popularity.) One day shortly after King Herod came out to speak to the people, he made an excellent speech (in the eyes of the audience). Let's see what happened to him:

> ...**because their country was nourished by the king's country** (obviously they received provision from him).
>
> **And upon a set day Herod, arrayed in royal apparel, sat upon his throne, and made an oration** (a speech) **unto them.**
>
> **And the people gave a shout, saying, It is the voice of a god, and not of a man.**
>
> Acts 12:20-22

King Herod came out with all of his fancy apparel on. After he finished talking, the people said, "This is the voice of a god; this is not the voice of a man. This is our god speaking." He made the mistake of not saying, *"No, I am not God. I am only a man. I am only a king appointed by men."* Instead, he allowed the imaginations of the people to run wild and allowed himself to be exalted above God in the eyes of the people. He neglected to restrain their vain thoughts. He actually allowed himself to be exalted above the knowing of God for his followers. He had been killing Christians for sport, and then allowed himself to be exalted in the imaginations of the people as God.

> **And immediately the angel of the Lord smote him, because he gave not God the glory: and he was eaten of worms, and gave up the ghost.**
>
> Acts 12:23

This is the king who had just killed James and was looking to kill Peter. He was perhaps saying to himself: "I am great. I am wonderful. I am exciting. Look at me. I've got it all together, don't I? Listen to me everyone, I will tell you great things." His speech was so wonderful to the people that the people imagined and exclaimed, "That is God." he did not restrain them, but probably thought, "Perhaps I am." That distorted imagination led him to his death.

Let's compare this incident to today. Even in ministry, the days of the superstar personalities are over. *God is to receive the glory for the work being done by the Holy Spirit in the Name of Jesus.* God's will is that every one of the kings as well as the people all over the world receive the Word of God and worship the King of kings and Lord of lords.

But the word of God grew and multiplied.
Acts 12:24

The king died, but the Word of God continued to multiply. God is no respecter of persons. (Acts 10:34.) God will *confirm* His Word in you when you exalt the Word. There is no force anywhere that can stop those who are exalting the Word of God. If you are holding up the Word of God in your thoughts and in your heart, and in your lifestyle, then God is with you. Your enemies may be rising up against you, but you will flourish, because of the Word of God in your life. The Word of God will act as a floatation device to keep you on top no matter what the enemy tries to do to you. So, the Word grew and multiplied, and the king went down in worms.

Anyone who comes against those exalting the Word of God is a fool. The Word *will* continue, and continue, and continue to grow!

How Do We See God?

For I say, through the grace given unto me, to every man that is among you, not to think of himself more highly than he ought to think; but to think

soberly, according as God hath dealt to every man the measure of faith.

Romans 12:3

Your thinking process, whether negative or positive, good or bad, has to do with what you have faith in. Do you remember how the children of Israel built a god from their own imagination? What did they build? A calf! Can you believe it, a calf. The calf was the graven image of their imagination of God. They had seen all the mighty miracles that God had done, yet their imagination of God and His provision was manifested in a golden cow. This was the image of what they could see in a fleshly sense from their own idea of what God was to them. So many of us have graven images of God in our own mind.

In America, some people due to some paintings and pictures only imagine Jesus as having blond hair and blue eyes. However, Jewish children many times are completely shocked when they come to this country for the first time and see blond hair and blue eyes, because they are not used to seeing that in Israel. Jesus was a Jew, so He was probably not the way we Americans imagine Him to be. We must be careful in every area of life not to give impressions by presenting images of our own imaginations of Who God is and Who He is not.

Look at it the Bible, as Paul teaches some superstitious people of Athens.

Forasmuch then as we are the offspring of God, we ought not to think that the Godhead is like unto gold, or silver, or stone, graven by art and man's device.

And the times of this ignorance God winked at; but now commandeth all men every where to repent.

Acts 17:29,30

It is perhaps time for us to make some changes as to the images we have made of God from our own imaginations and devices. Many people in many ways have formed an image of what God happens to be or looks like according to the imaginations of *their mind.* Unfortunately, that sometimes stifles their freedom to see God *as a God for all people,* and will limit their own potential of what they can do in Christ. God is not a calf (a cow). He is a Spirit. (John 4:24.)

6
Bringing Into Captivity Every Thought

In the area of casting down imaginations, remember that words are actually thought pictures. There is the saying that a picture is worth a thousand words, but I really believe that one word can be worth a thousand pictures. When you read these next few statements, you will begin to imagine some things.

"Dog." Certainly when you read that you don't just imagine the letters, "d-o-g." You see a dog. Each person who reads this will have a *different* imagination of what kind of dog, but we all see a dog. Some may see a cocker spaniel, others a German shepherd, etc. according to their imagination.

Let's clarify it. I will tell you what kind of dog. *"A black, curly-haired, floppy-eared dog."* Do you see him? As you read these words describing the dog, you had to throw out your own imagination and thoughts to put in the thoughts I gave you. That is just what Satan tries to do with you. He wants to *replace* the images of who God desires for you to be with his own words to present another image to you.

There is nothing necessarily wrong with the words I gave you. But words *form* an imagination and vision in your mind, and those thoughts must be captured, analyzed and checked with the Word of God.

> **Casting down imaginations, and every high thing
> that exalteth itself against the knowledge of God,** *and
> bringing into captivity every thought to the obedience
> of Christ.*
>
> **2 Corinthians 10:5**

If the words are not captured and checked, you
may incubate or hibernate the wrong seeds of
imagination in the comfortable soil of your mind. They
will grow to become a part of your life that you do not
want. Every thought is to be your prisoner until you
interrogate it as to its origin and purpose and motive
with the Word of God.

> **For the word of God is quick** (alive) **and powerful**
> (full of power), **and sharper than any twoedged sword,**
> **piercing even to** *the dividing asunder of the soul* (mind,
> will, and emotions) *and spirit* (human spirit), *and the
> joints and marrow* (flesh or body), *and is a discerner
> of the thoughts and intents of the heart.*
>
> *Hebrews 4:12*

Learn to cut your thoughts open with the Word
of God. Capture those thoughts, examine them, then
either reject or protect them.

The Whirlwind of Instability

> **Casting down imaginations, and every high thing
> that exalteth itself against the knowledge of God, and
> bringing into captivity every thought....**
>
> **2 Corinthians 10:5**

There is what I call a *whirlwind* (tornado) that goes
on in some of our minds. Whirlwinds are spawned
when hot and cold air come together. When hot and
cold air collide in the right conditions, a whirlwind is
started. Once given a chance to gain momentum, it will
grow to be a storm of terrific force, and anything that

gets in the middle of this whirlwind of hot and cold air is going to be changed, usually negatively.

Some of us have a whirlwind going on in our minds. Everything is confused and seems to be hitting the walls of our mind. Nothing is tied down, nothing is stable. We go from relationship to relationship, or from church to church, from thought to thought, from job to job; hot then cold, always finding something wrong with someone, or something else; if not the past, then the present, if not the present then the future. We are not pleased with our jobs, our families or any of our situations in life. We spawn a state of constant unstableness and confusion all around us, all the while still able to blurt out a systematic religious "Hallelujah." But inside, we are sick with that unstable feeling of uncertainty, because of our own imagination. James 1:8 says:

A double minded man is unstable in all his ways.

Look carefully at this scripture. It is not his ways that are making this man's mind unstable, but it is his double-mindedness that is making his ways unstable. Unstable ways are the result of double-mindedness, hot then cold coming together regarding the Word of God. That is the way of the world, not of God.

Stress, depression, worry or fear in the life of a Christian are all due to a double-minded way of thinking. On one hand the person sees and hears the Word of God and gets excited; then old thoughts and imaginations of the past, fears of the future or circumstances or situations, begin to crowd out faith in the Word, and the person begins to *vacillate* back and forth between fear and faith; hot then cold, cold then hot. Fear of circumstances and situations entering in your mind will nullify your faith, and if not cast down immediately *will* render the Word of God useless.

Some people allow their imaginations to go so wild that you can see the result on their faces. You can see worry, fear, grief, hurt, disappointment and concern for financial problems. A person's countenance reveals what is going on within him. You can also see joy, peace and happiness, too. This is the one area that God cannot control. It's up to you to rise up and take control of this area. You can put a halt on the whirlwind in your mind any time you want to according to the Word of God, with the help of the Holy Spirit (which is the power of God).

Taking Control of Thoughts

I have outlined how to cast down negative thoughts with a five-step process outlined in the last chapter of this book. To do this, you must present yourself just as you are and start taking control right where you are in life. **For as he thinketh in his heart, so is he....** (Prov. 23:7). That puts you in control. This is so exciting, because *you can change your thought process any time you want.* You can stop thinking on non-productive imaginations today.

In my early years as a Christian, I remember that I was always trying to make my life work *my way*, while trying to figure out where I was going and what I was supposed to be doing. No one ever told me that I needed to get my mind renewed to the Word of God or that I needed to start renewing my thoughts. No one ever told me I could *cast down* those negative thoughts I was entertaining. However, later I found out in the Bible that I could renew my mind and cast down the thoughts captivating me.

Mind science and the theory of mind over matter does not work in God's system. It must always be the Word of God and faith over every situation to have consistent victory.

This is a scripture that you need to underline in your Bible and study:

> **For I know the thoughts that I think toward you, saith the Lord, thoughts of peace** [not the tornado, not the confusion], **and not of evil, to give you an expected end.**
>
> **Jeremiah 29:11**

We are created to be able to expect something. Begin to expect to receive something good, get a vision for something happening in your life based on the Word of God. We should be *ready* to receive whatever God has for us. Expect to receive blessings from God when you pray. This is to be your "expected end." There is nothing or no one that can stop you from being the best you can be, but you. Believe me, *there is nothing to stop you*, but you. God is not trying to, and the devil doesn't have the power to, unless you let him. That leaves you in control!

> **Now unto him that is able to do exceeding *abundantly* above all that we ask or think, according to *the power that worketh in us.***
>
> **Ephesians 3:20**

Start thinking higher thoughts in God.

Do you realize that research has proven that you and I use only about 10% of our brain capability? Scientists believe that the average person is capable of speaking 200 languages fluently. You have a lot of *potential* with the Word of God and the Spirit of God working in you.

I made a decision before I got married. I decided that the word "divorce" would not be in my vocabulary. In the early part of our marriage my wife and I got into a heated *"I'm going to leave and go to my mother's house to live"* discussion. Kathy and I both knew that her mother lived in California, 1,000 miles away, but she packed up everything and put it into her car. She put our oldest daughter Monet (then two years old) in her safety car seat and took off out of the driveway on her way. I said, "Okay. Have fun at your mother's house."

Neither Kathy nor I wanted this to happen. As she drove off, I said, "I'll be here when you come back." She really didn't want to go to her mother's. She didn't want to go anywhere. She really wanted me to change from the way I was acting, and rightfully so. She was going to make a point with me: "I'm upset and you should know it."

I quickly got into my car and tried to follow her. I spotted her driving downtown. I saw her go down one street, then she saw me and went over the railroad tracks with the baby's head bouncing as she made her getaway. This went on for about 15 minutes all over the downtown section of our city, until Kathy finally stopped and we began to talk about what was really bothering her. Within a few minutes we ended up laughing about the whole thing. It was one of the funniest scenes ever.

It is important to deal with the *thoughts* going on deep down inside of us quickly. My wife had thoughts in her mind, and we had situations that needed to be

dealt with and reconciled. There are other thoughts
that we cannot allow to occupy space in our minds at
all, because if *planted* in the proper environment, they
will cause a world of problems. We should not waste
our brain power on these negative thoughts. We must
learn to throw them out to be successful in life. If you
will consciously say to yourself, "That thought is not
according to the will and the purpose of God for me,
so I cast it down," your thoughts will begin to change.
But the only way to do this, as I have stated before,
is by knowing what the Word of God says.

Think On These Things

> **Finally, brethren, whatsoever things are true,
> whatsoever things are honest, whatsoever things are
> just, whatsoever things are pure, whatsoever things
> are lovely, whatsoever things are of good report; if
> there be any virtue, and if there be any praise, think
> on these things.**
>
> **Phillipians 4:8**

Some of us dwell on negative reports; it's our
lifestyle. Anything that is true, lovely and of a good
report, think on those things. Our minds will be
occupied by something all of the time. Why not think
on the good rather than the bad? We know that there
are negative reports. We are not going to close our eyes
to the problems and things that need to be dealt with,
but we were *not built to keep* all the problems of the
world in our mind.

Casting down imaginations begins when you first
throw down the things that you would normally think
and begin inserting the things that God thinks; and
to think truly great thoughts we must think the
God-kind of thoughts, and the God-kind of thoughts

are expressed in God's book, the Bible. Forsake your thoughts, get hold of God's thoughts. You then will be able to do greater things. *You must allow new thoughts to be birthed into your heart and mind.*

Saturate yourself with the Word of God and watch the seeds grow inside of you as you give place to the birthing process of new ideas according to the will of God. To complete the CDI process, you must plant the Word of God in every area where the evil thoughts have been cast out. The next chapter outlines a five-step process on how to do just that using the Word of God. Once you begin to cast down those negative imaginations and start exalting the knowledge of God, God is going to give you a new vision. Start this process *today.* You will see yourself doing something different, exciting and fruitful.

The five-step CDI process outlined in this final chapter is a five-step process designed to help you win in every situation in life by utilizing the Word of God.

7

The Five-Step CDI Process

Outlined in this final chapter is a five-step process given to me for the Body of Christ by the Holy Spirit, designed to help you to *win* in every battle or situation in your daily life and to help change your lifestyle from defeat, fear, complacency and stagnation by utilizing the *Word of God, prayer, and the direction of the Holy Spirit to cast down imaginations and exalt the Word of God.*

STEP 1
Receiving

As we have learned in the previous chapters of this book, the first step is *receiving.* You must be ready to receive those ideas, thoughts or suggestions that line up with God's will and purpose for your life according to His Word. As well, you must be ready to *reject* and *cast down* those ideas, thoughts or suggestions that can be detrimental to your growth as a Christian. Your first step in the CDI process is to receive. You will receive information all of the time, but *you can control* what you receive.

Let me give you an example. Television is one of the most exciting tools the Body of Christ has available to spread the Gospel, and the Gospel is being preached on certain channels at certain times. However, if you were to watch television in your home on some channels, you would find programs that are not desirable for a Christian to watch at all. The choice of what you receive is dependent on what channel you *choose* to tune in on your receiver. You don't have to stop watching television altogether, just tune into the programs that will benefit your life.

As a born-again believer, you cannot allow fear to stop you from being in a receiving posture. *Being ready to receive is vitally important to your growth as a Christian.* Second Timothy 1:7 states,

> **For God hath *not* given us the *spirit of fear*. . . .**

Notice, fear is a spirit, and you must come against that spirit of fear, bind that spirit of fear and cast that spirit down out of your mind in order to be ready to *freely* receive, or the spirit of fear will rule and reign in your life above the knowledge of God. Second Timothy 1:7 also states,

> **For God hath not given us the spirit of fear; but of power, and of love, and of a *sound mind*.**

STEP 2
Analyzing

The second step in the CDI process is the process of *analyzing* what you have received. For many Christians, this step is clouded by the often-asked question: "Analyze what with what?" Let me answer this valid question this way: Second Corinthians 10:5 states:

> **. . . and bringing into captivity *every thought to the obedience of Christ*.**

Can you see it now?

To be effective in winning the battles you are faced with every day in life, you must *capture* (make prisoner) *every thought* (yes, every thought) that comes to your mind and analyze it in comparison to its obedience (or lack of obedience) to God's will in your life, before you act on it.

The Bible states in John 1:14 that Jesus is the Word made flesh. It is up to you to take every thought prisoner, but remember *you* must do this. God will not do it for you. He has given you every weapon you need to make wise decisions in every area of life based on His Word. (You, too, must become the Word wrapped in flesh dwelling on this earth.)

This step, of all the steps in this five-step process, is where many Christians get clouded in their brain, because they don't know what the Word of God says regarding obedience. Most people know only Bible stories and abstract information about the bible, but many people think it is impossible to know how to live a lifestyle as a Christian according to the Bible. They have not been taught to *capture* the thoughts of their minds in light of the Word of God. They try to do it from a cultural or worldly view with no reference to the Bible to back up the standards. Simply put, they know the traditions of men, their religious creed, sectarian statements or cultural beliefs, but they don't *truly* know the Word of God and how to apply it to their everyday situations. That simply will not work!

The scripture says, "to the obedience of Christ," and that is what it means. You must be ready to find out what the Bible says about *each* area you are dealing with, not what Brother so and so thinks the Bible said about that area, or what you thought you heard the preacher say one day about that area. *You must know for yourself* what the Word of God says about that area, or suggestion, thought or idea that has been presented to your mind. If you don't know what is in obedience to Christ in that area concerning that thought, then one of two things will result, both equally negative.

Perhaps you will out of ignorance of the Word of God and *fear of exalting* the wrong thing, cast down a thought, idea or suggestion that *is* in obedience to the Word of God and miss out on the promises and blessings associated with it; or you will, through ignorance of the will of God and what the Word of God says, exalt a negative idea, thought or suggestion. This idea, thought or suggestion will pass the analytical test in your mind because of ignorance as being in obedience to Christ. You will then put it into your mind and begin to accept it as a part of your lifestyle. It will be to your detriment simply because of a lack of knowledge of the Word of God.

In Hosea 4:6 the Lord says:

> **My people are destroyed for lack of knowledge: because thou has rejected knowledge, I will also reject thee, that thou shalt be no priest to me: seeing thou hast forgotten the law of thy God, I will also forget thy children.**

Your ignorance of the Word of God may be hurting you, your family and your children.

Part of the training for an FBI counterfeit specialist is first to perfect the study of the pattern and makeup of true, legitimate U.S. currency. This is done long before specialists attempt to compare their knowledge to the discerning of counterfeit bills. Like the FBI, you must first become proficient in *knowing* the Word of God, then you will be ready to rightly divide the Word of God from the lies of the devil submitted to you. If you are unsure about analyzing thoughts, suggestions or ideas, then determine to *learn to rightly divide the Word of truth.*

STEP 3
Accepting or Rejecting

The third step is also a crucial pivot point in the entire CDI process. Once you have received and analyzed the information, thought, suggestion or idea that has been presented to you, *you must now do something with it. You must and will either accept it or reject it,* there is no middle ground about this. Either one or the other will happen, no matter how you try to avoid it. In Revelation 3:15 Jesus said to the angel of the church of Laodicea:

I know thy works, that thou art neither cold nor hot: I would thou wert cold or hot.

So then because thou art lukewarm, and neither cold nor hot, I will spue (spit) thee out of my mouth.

You will have to decide if you are cold or hot regarding each idea, thought or suggestion that is presented to you. You will have to learn how to spew some things out of your mind in order to grow in the things of God; that's just the way it is.

One of the hardest things for Christians to do is to realize they must reject some of the thoughts, suggestions or ideas from some well-meaning people in their life. Some of these people may be very close, perhaps a close relative or a long-time friend or religious associate who has been suggesting some things that don't line up with the will of God expressed in the Word of God. Rejecting these suggestions at first is very hard, but you must understand that you will have to learn how to be either hot or cold on an idea, suggestion or thought, all based upon the Word of God. Lukewarm won't do. That *must* be treated as if it were cold.

As you make your decision, let me help you to see what happens with that idea, thought or suggestion that you are dealing with by explaining it this way: *If the idea, thought or suggestion meets the test through analyzing it with and through the Word of God, normally all rejection efforts will be dropped at that time. It is then accepted and will become a part of the stronghold (as another brick in building a fortified wall) as you protect that part of your lifestyle, knowing its foundation is the Word of God. Eventually, over time, that thought or idea that has been accepted will become a part of the wall protecting a part of your lifestyle, thoughts, morals and actions.*

The sad part about this process is that many Christians with a lack of knowledge of the Word of God become stifled with the negative ideas, thoughts or suggestions that they have accepted over the years. They receive undesirable results, because what they are exalting is not according to the Word of God. Over time, as these people build strongholds in their minds, brick by brick, suggestion by suggestion, idea by idea, thought by thought, those negative, untrue thoughts, ideas and suggestions become exalted over the truth of the Word of God, making the Word of God of none effect, as they become hardened and fortified, just as though they were the Word of God.

This process (accepting or rejecting) is really not new at all, it has been going on since the creation. However, many Christians don't seem to know that they can be victorious in this process in their daily lives. Every believer has been given authority over this area in the Name of Jesus. However, you must use God's weapons to be successful in tearing down these strongholds. Your weapons are the sword of the Spirit, the Word of God. (Eph. 6:17.)

Your physical efforts won't work. **For the weapons of our warfare are not carnal, but mighty *through God* to the pulling down of *strongholds*** [thought castles]; **Casting down imaginations....** (2 Cor. 10:4,5). You see, the *only way* you can know how to cast down thought castles (strongholds) in your mind is through God, not through any carnal or fleshly means. Trying to do this in the flesh or in your own power is like trying to break down a physical brick wall with your bare hands. It is impossible without using the right tools. God knows you'll need a spiritual jackhammer, a sledgehammer, a bulldozer, a crane and a wrecking ball to make the needed changes in your life, and He has all of these things you need to cast down the negative thought castles in your mind and reestablish the Word of God in its place.

I'd like to explain it this way. To get things on the right track, you must be willing to take out the weapons that God has given you to cast down those thoughts that you are holding on to (maybe secretly) *by rejecting those things that do not meet the standards of a lifestyle based on the Word of God.* Next, be ready to *exalt* the Word of God in that area, tearing down that old thought in comparison with the living Word of God.

Here's a practical suggestion: Make a point to take time to sit down with a piece of paper and a pencil or pen and examine yourself, writing down changes that you need to make. Be ready to accept or reject some of your ways and protected thoughts in light of the Word of God. Do this before you move on to expand into any new ground in your life. Remember, you must do this with the *willingness* to change, or it will do no good at all. Let's now move on to the next step, replacing.

STEP 4
Replacing

After the first three steps in the CDI process, you probably feel as if you are making some progress. Perhaps you have discovered and cast down some things you may have been thinking about yourself or others that were not right, or maybe something you were doing that was not according to the Word of God, and these things have now been cast down, repented of and removed. Though these are bold and noble steps, stopping after only the first three steps in the CDI process will only ensure eventual defeat. This is where most Christians get stagnated in their Christian life. They have completed all the don'ts, but know nothing about the do's. Step 4, *replacing*, will ensure that you will continue to grow as a Christian and continue to change as you receive God's promises.

First, before we explore this area, you must decide in your mind that living daily as a Christian is the type of *lifestyle* you want beginning today, and for the remainder of your life. Casting negative thoughts, idea and suggestions out of your mind, is one thing, but you can't operate your life on emptiness, vacancy or in a rejection state. Some day you are going to have to *occupy* that space with something that is positive and according to the will of God in order to win. As a child of God, you must be ready to *replace* old thoughts, ideas and suggestions with God's Word.

Let's review up to now. We discussed that once the thought or idea is received, it is then analyzed. When that thought is analyzed and found not to meet the standards in the Word of God, it is then rejected, and that empty place must be filled with the Word of God. Learn now to remember to replace each negative thought, idea or suggestion *with the Word of God with which you used to analyze it.* By doing so, *you allow those scriptures to become the new standard in your lifestyle* in that area for the rest of your life. *That now becomes your confession of faith!* You are confessing God's promises that will come to pass for you in that area.

In Psalms 119:89, the Bible states

For ever, O Lord, thy word is settled in heaven.

Learn to settle your matters with the Word of God, because *the Word of God is already settled.* Remembering to replace the negative thoughts with the promises of God will ensure that you will always keep yourself growing in the Word of God, settled in the things of God and not the whims of the world's ideas.

STEP 5
Renewing

I beseech *you* therefore, brethren, by the mercies of God, that ye present your bodies a living sacrifice, holy, acceptable unto God, which is *your reasonable service.*

And be not conformed to this world, but be *ye* transformed by *the renewing of your mind,* **that ye may** *prove* **what is that good, and acceptable, and perfect,** *will of God.*

Romans 12:1,2

For some Christians, memorizing scriptures is not a very hard task to accomplish. However, in our final step in the five-step CDI process we will find that just having head knowledge of the Word of God alone *will not change* your lifestyle. This is the area that has to do with religion. Many people think that it is a compliment to be called religious.

Being called religious is really not a compliment at all. Jesus dealt with many *religious* leaders of His day. To be religious simply means to continually do the same thing. For example, most people religiously go to work in the morning. Like a ritual, they get up at the same time and do the same things every morning to prepare themselves to get into the same car that they always drive down the same road at the same time to the same building and punch the same clock at the same factory or sign in at the same office, day after day, *religiously!* But, these same people if offered a job across the street paying a little bit more would quit their present job in a moment, because they are *not committed* to that company even though they have been doing the same thing day after day, week after week, month after month, year after year religiously. They are just religious. Many people treat the Word of God the same way. They recite the same scriptures with the same lack of faith and get the same old negative results no matter what.

To be successful in growing in the things of God, you must accept the fact that you are to be renewing your mind to the Word of God every day, not just going through a religious routine to be seen of men. When it comes to the CDI process, you can do all of the first four steps and end up frustrated and religious if Step No. 5, *renewing your mind,* is not included. Learn now to renew your mind. Meditate and observe to *do.* It is not enough just to know the Word of God, *but your lifestyle must be known by you doing the Word of God.* Become a living example of God's Word in your life, your word and your deed. It's your decision.

You can become victorious and more effective for the Kingdom of God, by learning to cast down negative imaginations and exalt the Word of God. Decide today to: **Step 1** *Receive;* **Step 2** *Analyze;* **Step 3** *Reject or Accept (cast down or fortify);* **Step 4** *Replace (with the Word of God);* and **Step 5** *Renew Your Mind.* My life and the lives of many others have completely changed, and so will yours as you begin this daily process.

About the Author

Don Shorter is founder and pastor of the Word of Faith Christian Center in Tacoma, Washington.

His teachings on living a lifestyle of victory is personified in his lifestyle teachings and his instructions in the CDI process (casting down imaginations), based on 2 Corinthians 10:4,5. Don has a saying that if something is started in the Spirit, it will be sustained by the Spirit; if something is started in the flesh, it must be sustained by the flesh.''

While in secular broadcasting and the fast life of music and entertainment, Don became disoriented and discouraged on the verge of suicide, while running from the call of God on His life.

Because of the prayers of his wife, Kathy, and others, Don soon made a decision to totally commit his life to the Lord, accepting His call as a pastor and teacher, he now teaches the Word of God around the world.

Prior to becoming a pastor, Don worked as National Public Relations Director for John Jacobs and the Power Team, along with assisting other prominent ministries with their public relations and media.

Don and his wife of nearly 20 years, Kathy, share their lives with three lovely children: Monet, Dawnet and Donald, Jr.

On December 18, 1988, the Holy Spirit spoke to Don to start a church, beginning with him and his family (then only four), promising that He would add to it. Since that time, God has multiplied the ministry to nearly 1,000, and growing with outreaches to the Philippines, and soon South Africa, Australia and Mexico.

Don and Kathy have an effective television ministry seen by thousands; teaching the Word of God in a practical way.

Don and Kathy's teaching tapes and videos covering a wide range of subjects and are being used throughout America, and around the world.

For a complete list of tapes, videos and printed materials by Don and Kathy Shorter, write to:

Don Shorter
Word of Faith World Wide Ministries
P.O. Box 44051
Tacoma, WA 98444

**Available from your local bookstore
or by writing:**

Harrison House
P. O. Box 35035 • Tulsa, OK 74153

Don and Kathy Shorter are thankful to God for calling them to be a dynamic teaching team. Through the ministry of the Word Don and Kathy often witness many, many, miracles of healing and restoration to peoples lives through the Word and gifts of healing during their meetings. Through their calling to teach the anointed Word of God, faith arises in the hearts of the people making way for great victories.

Their lifestyle teaching approach has allowed their ministry to include many diverse areas of ministry to many diverse types of people, including their "Principles in Marriage Seminars" for couples, "Leadership in Ministry Training" for pastors and leaders, "Christian Lifestyle Classes" involving a diversity of areas, and specialized ministry to men and women through their "Women of Wealth" and "Men's Perspective" meetings. Pastor Don and Kathy Shorter are committed to ministering healing, help, teaching salvation and deliverance to the Body of Christ and the unchurched world wide.

Cassette Tapes by Donald Shorter, Sr.

BOOKS OF THE BIBLE:
Romans Chapter 1
Romans Chapter 2
Romans Chapter 3
Romans Chapter 4
Romans Chapter 5
Romans Chapter 6
Romans Chapter 7
Romans Chapter 8
Romans Chapter 9
Romans Chapter 10
Philippians Part 1
Philippians Part 2
Philippians Part 3
23rd Psalms

EFFECTIVE MINISTERING:
Give Up, Give In, Give Out
The Substance of Faith
Healing That Maintains

LIFESTYLE SERIES:
Family Cornerstone Of Life
Successful Marriage Principles
Power Of Your Words
Birthing Your Future
5 Steps to Financial Freedom
Living In the Image of Your God
Following the Voice of God

SPIRITUAL WARFARE:
Casting Down Imaginations
Renewing the Mind
The Power In You
The Force of Joy

Video Tapes by Donald Shorter, Sr.
Power in You, Part 2
The Force of Joy, Part 5
The Power of Prayer, Part 1

Books by Donald Shorter, Sr.
Casting Down Imaginations
The Power In You

Cassette Tapes by Kathy Shorter
Stepping Into a New Realm
Breaking Controlling Habits

Available From:
WORD OF FAITH WORLDWIDE MINISTRIES
P.O. Box 44051   Tacoma, WA 92444   (206) 536-0801